transferred

how to add original images to everything
from fabrics to ceramics

Isabel de Cordova
Photography by Sue Wilson

conran
OCTOPUS

contents

RIGHT *Star anise is a beautiful
spice that looks great
transferred on to shot glasses.*

introduction

Transferred images are the latest way to decorate your home. Whether you want to put some patterns on your bed linen, or capture the colours of autumnal leaves on a lampshade, transfers let you personalize your home in a unique and stylish way. You can use photographs, line drawings, music, letters and even real flowers and leaves as your subjects, just look around for inspiration.

The aim of this book is to show how to transform everyday objects, from tableware to cushions, and even computer mouse mats, into stunning individual originals. By using transfers you can customize a variety of surfaces, including fabric, ceramics, metal, wood, plastic, stone and glass. You can do as little or much as you like – whether you want to create an eye-catching centrepiece for a table, an accent piece for the living room or even a matching set of curtains, cushions and bed linen to create a total theme for a room.

As you wander around the shops and flick through lifestyle magazines you will see that photographic images have been applied to a wide variety of products and that the use of transfers in decoration has become a very popular style in recent years. This is an easy way to create a new look in your home.

The great advantage of using transfers is that the techniques involved are very easy and you do not need to be an artist as there is no drawing involved. The process is simple and provides an easy way to personalize household items – whether for your own use or as unique gifts to give to friends and family. Some projects are more time-consuming than others – it will take longer to make the Curtains of falling petals (see page 22) than the Fishbowl vase (see page 54), for example – and some are a little fiddly, but all are quite simple.

One of the best things about transferring is that it allows you to use personal photographs and images. I love the idea of being able to display pictures in an interesting way. You could put pictures of your family on coffee mugs or a child's drawing on a bedside lamp. But if you'd rather keep your holiday snaps in a drawer, then transferring can still be for you. There are plenty of inanimate images that would make ideal transfers. You could, for example, photocopy a flower or a leaf and use that as your transferred image. The end of the book features some of the images I used to make the projects featured in this book. Just remember though, that you don't have to use them, you can use any image you like. Transferring is a very personal technique, so you should think carefully and choose images that suit your individual style.

There are sixteen projects in this book, each with clear step-by-step instructions covering all the different ways to transfer an image. Once you have got the feel for them, I hope you will feel inspired to experiment further on your own.

ISABEL DE CORDOVA

getting started

materials and surfaces

You can transfer images on to all sorts of materials, allowing you to decorate your home and make inventive personalized gifts. Throughout the book you will find examples of all the various transferring techniques, plus details of the surfaces for which they are suitable. Here is a quick reference guide to the various methods.

There are a number of ways to transfer an image on to a surface, but the basic theory remains the same. Colour photocopy your chosen image on to the shiny side of some transfer paper. There are then various methods of attaching the transfer paper to surfaces such as ceramic, glass, fabric, wood, metal, paper and plastic.

The linen shoe bag is the only project not to use transfer paper, using transfer paste to move ink from a colour photocopy on to fabric instead.

You will find suppliers for the wet release transfer paper and the transfer paste on page 96.

Transferring methods

Simple wet release transfer paper

This method can be used on paper, plastic, glass, ceramics, fabric covered canvases, and metal. Simply immerse the transfer paper images in water or dab them with a wet sponge, then slide off the backing paper and attach the picture to your chosen surface. Glass, metal and ceramic can then be baked in a warm oven to further secure the transfers, but they will not be dishwasherproof.

Wet release transfer paper with turpentine

This method can be used on paper, plastic, wood and stone. It is done by applying a thin layer of turpentine to the surface where the transfer will go and then applying the wet release transfer paper.

If the surface is quite rough, part-fill a pump action spray with turpentine and lightly mist the transfer. This helps the image melt into the nooks and crannies.

Wet release transfer paper with glue

Used on absorbent surfaces such as canvas and paper, this method is the same as the wet release transfer paper method except for the fact that a thin layer of 50 per cent water-diluted PVA glue is brushed on to the surface before the transfers are applied. The glue helps the transfers to stick to absorbent surfaces and also makes it easier to adjust the position of the transfers.

Iron-on wet release transfer paper

This method also uses wet release transfer paper, but involves ironing the image on to fabric. The backing paper is then soaked off to reveal the transfer. Since the image is applied to the fabric face down, you will need to flip the image before you begin if you do not want it to appear back-to-front.

Epson iron-on transfer paper

This method allows a transfer to be ironed straight on to fabric. The backing paper is then gently peeled off. Unfortunately, Epson paper can only be used with Epson printers, but it lets you print computer scans straight on to transfer paper. If you do not have a computer, scanner and Epson printer, use the iron-on wet release transfer paper method instead.

Transfer paste

This method is for use on natural fibre fabric only. Put a piece of foil under the fabric before starting. Lay a trimmed colour photocopied image on another piece of foil then, with the image face up, spread transfer paste over the picture. Place the image face down on the fabric and press down to ensure it has fixed. Remove any excess paste, then leave to dry.

Use a sponge to soak the backing paper with water then use your fingertip to gently rub away the backing paper, leaving the image clearly revealed. Leave the transfer to dry then apply another coat of paste to seal the image.

Surface texture

Generally speaking, it is easiest to transfer images on to smooth textured materials. With fabric the best results are achieved when transfers are applied to even weaves, and consequently fabrics with a raised texture, such as towelling or velvet, are not suitable for transfers. Fortunately, using wet release transfer paper with turpentine (see page 10) allows other materials with a slight surface texture, such as wood and stone, to be used as the turpentine makes the transfers melt into the contours of the surface.

Surface colour

Since they are slightly transparent, transfers usually work best on a light-coloured background. A dark background will inevitably show through the transfer. This effect can sometimes be used to deliberately incorporate the background into the picture, as shown on the Rose cushion (see page 38) and the Take-away tray (see page 62). Do remember though that a coloured transfer on a coloured background will result in a third colour. If you are not sure what will result from your colour mixes, it is wise to test the transfer on a like-coloured background before you embark on the real project.

Fabric transfer aftercare

In most cases a fabric item can be given a gentle hand-wash or be laundered using a delicate cycle. However, always check the transfer manufacturer's instructions first. Turn the item inside-out before washing or place it in a fabric bag to protect the image. After washing an article, iron it carefully to fix the images, remembering to lay a piece of baking parchment over the image to protect it and prevent it from melting. Do not fold the transfers for storage as this may cause them to crack.

where to find your images

Choosing an image to transfer can be a tricky business. Sometimes an image will present itself as an ideal candidate, but usually you have to really hunt around. Photographs can be a great source of images, but try to think beyond them to include line drawings, wallpaper, fabric patterns, music, handwriting and even two-dimensional objects like leaves and feathers.

Choosing an image

Images on any material that can be photocopied or scanned and printed from a computer can be transferred. There are endless possibilities and you can start by looking around your home for some inspiration. Look through books and magazines, and old photographs too. Other good source materials can be letters, music scores, memorabilia, children's drawings, paintings, buttons, and natural textures. Look outside and search for leaves and flowers, feathers, shells and pebbles. You might want to create a theme, based perhaps on a favourite hobby or pastime, such as sport or music.

Copyright

Always make sure that the images you use for transferring are not copyrighted. Using postcards or greeting cards from art galleries and elsewhere, for example, is not advisable. It is easy to tell whether the copyright of an image is owned by an individual or a company because it will feature the symbol © plus the owner's name either in the corner, on the reverse or – in the case of an extended publication – in a list of credits and acknowledgements. Fortunately, there are publications available that provide copyright-free images that can be copied for personal use (see page 96).

image styles and manipulation

Once you have chosen an image, there are a number of ways you can manipulate it, should you so desire. You can, of course, use the original image, but if you're feeling a little more creative there are plenty of other options.

Reducing and enlarging

Altering the size of an image is an easy way to ring the changes if you intend to use it more than once on a project. Side by side a small and large version of an image can make a charming composition. By using a photocopier or computer scanner, you can reduce or enlarge your pictures to suit your design. Remember though that if you increase the size of your image by more than 100 per cent, you will begin to notice a reduction in the quality of the picture, particularly if it includes a high level of fine detail. Similarly, if you drastically reduce the size of a picture, the details will begin to merge.

Repeat images

Deliberately repeating an image is an easy way to bring a cohesive element to your design. The effect will vary according to the way you place the repeated images. Multiple images can look quite intense on a small object, such as on the plate opposite with leaves fanning out around its edge, but when teamed with the less structured design of the plate below from the same set, its intensity is toned down and works as a unifying design element.

When placed at regular intervals, a repeated image becomes a pattern. If you're going to do this, think carefully about where you want to place the transferred images and calculate how many copies you will need. Make a few extra, just in case.

Overlapping images

You can use the slightly translucent nature of transfer paper to your advantage when laying down your images. By overlapping the transfers you can create a multi-layered image. This technique works best when used sparingly or the pictures can become quite confused. Nevertheless, it is ideal for illustrating delicate images, such as the skeletal leaves shown on these plates.

If your chosen transferred images are coloured, overlapping them will result in further variations of colour. Get it right and this can produce jewel-like effects. If you are unsure how well colours will work when overlapped, experiment on a similar-coloured surface before you begin.

Tints

If you have access to a computer scanner you will be able to alter the colour of your chosen images. You can also do this on a colour photocopier, though the range of possible colour variations will be more limited. If the project on which you're working needs to fit in with the colour scheme of a room, for example, this means that you can adapt your image to suit. So, whether you prefer subtle complementary colour variations or bold, eye-catching colours, you can adapt your images to suit your taste.

Flipping images

Another way to add variety to your transfers is to flip the original pictures. If you want to do this you will need access to a computer, scanner and colour printer, as a photocopier does not allow you to flip images. The resulting mirror image can be used to add variety to your designs. Placing mirror-images side by side is a dramatic way to make a feature of flipped pictures. It draws the eye to their meeting point and gives an impression of regularity and order.

Some of the projects in this book, such as those that use iron-on methods or transfer paste, flip images as part of the transferring process. This does not usually matter unless the picture contains elements that you particularly want to appear the correct way round. Think carefully about the images you use in these instances as images containing text, people and buildings, for example, might need to be flipped before they are transferred.

Adjoining images

If your design incorporates more than one transfer, you may well need to master the technique of laying them down edge to edge. Both the simple wet release transfer paper method and the wet release transfer paper with turpentine method allow you to adjust the position of transfers when you first apply them. The best way to achieve a neat fit in this case is to place the transfer close to its final position and then to slide it gently into place. Iron-on methods require a little more precision as you will need to make sure that the edges of transfers are precisely aligned before you apply the iron.

When ironing a design in place, it can be tricky to ensure that all the edges have adhered to the fabric. When ironing transfers edge to edge, take care not to iron over an uncovered image as it will melt and stick to the base of your iron. A double layer of baking parchment can be used as a temporary barrier between the iron and existing transfers.

Spot colour

If you do not have access to a computer and scanner, there are still ways to dramatically alter specific elements of pictures. The plate opposite shows a picture in the bottom right-hand corner that has been altered to make it seem as though the little girl is wearing a bright orange dress. This dramatic effect is actually quite simple to achieve.

First trace the outline of the dress on to some tracing paper, then photocopy the black and white picture and a square of your chosen colour on to some transfer paper. Place the traced dress over the square of coloured transfer paper and use it as a template to cut out a coloured dress shape. Use a piece of masking tape to stop the image slipping once you have begun cutting.

When you have attached the black and white transfer to the plate, transfer the coloured dress shape on top. This result is a limited area of colour on an otherwise black and white image.

Sepia

If you use sepia film in your camera, you will find that your photographs have an atmosphere that colour pictures lack. Perhaps it is because they hark back to a bygone era, but sepia images look fantastic when transferred on to household items as they seem to capture a mood as much as an image.

I particularly like to place sepia images next to ordinary black and white images, as shown opposite. If you have access to a computer, scanner and printer, you can manipulate ordinary photographs to take on a sepia tint.

projects

Fill your window with petals

cascading down from the ceiling to the floor. These delicate gauze curtains work as a discreet screen, bringing both privacy and style. As the sun shines through them, the curtains cast a hint of the petals' warm colour over your room.

Try to fit as many copies of the petals on to the transfer paper as possible – you will be surprised how many you will need. To add an extra creative dimension, you could enlarge and reduce the original petal a fraction to give you different sizes with which to work.

I chose this cascading effect because of the way it draws the eye down the curtain. To do this, place a few petals near the top of the curtains and then arrange the rest in a random pattern as though falling from the ceiling. At the very bottom of the curtains, position a few petals on their sides – as if they have reached the ground and settled there.

Hang your curtains in a window that receives the morning sun, open the window slightly to allow the breeze to waft through the fabric, and their full fairytale quality will be brought to life.

curtains of falling petals

You will need

Materials

Pressed petals or pictures of petals
   (see page 87)
Access to a colour photocopier
Lazertran transfer paper
Scalpel and cutting mat, or pair
   of scissors
Pair of sheer 100 per cent cotton
   curtains
Masking tape
Ironing board
Iron
Small shallow bowl
Sponge
Baking parchment

Technique

Iron-on wet-release transfer paper
   (see page 10)

1 First decide whether you want to photocopy real petals, or the pictures of petals on page 87. Try to fit as many petals on to one sheet of paper as possible – you could use a computer and scanner to aid this process, or you could colour photocopy the petals a number of times, then cut them out and stick them on a blank sheet of paper. Bear in mind that the images will appear flipped on the finished curtains. Colour copy the sheet of petals on to the shiny side of a sheet of transfer paper, then carefully cut them out using either a scalpel on a cutting mat, or a pair of scissors. To decide on the position of the petals, lay the first curtain flat on a table and roughly secure the images with pieces of masking tape (see page 48). Once you are happy with the position of the petals, place the curtain on an ironing board. One at a time, turn the petals face down (flipping the images) and, using a warm iron and a circular motion, press them into position. Continue until all the pieces are secure.

2 Lay the curtain on a clean waterproof surface. Fill a small shallow bowl with some water, then sponge water on to the petal transfer's backing paper. When the water has been absorbed and the paper looks less opaque, it will begin to lift off or curl back. Gently peel off the backing paper from the transfer and sponge off any excess white glue. Repeat this process with the rest of the petals.

3 Once the fabric is dry, lay the curtains on the ironing board with the images face up. Place a piece of baking parchment on top of the first few petals. Then, using a warm iron and a circular motion, as before, iron the fabric for a couple of minutes to seal the transfers. Take care not to accidentally iron over an uncovered image as it will melt and stick to the base of the iron. Continue until the images sink into the fabric. (The curtains should be ironed in this way, using the baking parchment, every time they are washed, as this will secure the transfers.) Repeat the process with the second curtain.

Transform a favourite picture

into a unique work of art by transferring it on to some stretched canvas. Whether you choose a family picture or even a holiday scene, this stylish project lets you add a personal touch to the photographs you display around your home.

Since the canvas becomes such a feature of the project, it has no need for a picture frame and the final result would certainly merit a place

canvas art

on your mantelpiece. If you use a sepia picture you will find that it will fit well in a traditional or modern setting, a grand house or a modest flat.

Transferring on to canvas is an extremely easy process, and once you have mastered it you could well be inspired to make a whole set of prints for your living room. A nice idea is to make some extra copies to give to your friends and family as gifts to remember a special occasion.

You will need

Materials

Acrylic-primed linen canvas – stretched
    over a wooden frame

Sepia photograph

Access to a colour photocopier

Lazertran transfer paper

Scalpel, metal ruler and cutting mat,
    or pair of scissors

Large shallow tray

Newspaper

50 per cent water-diluted PVA glue

Large paintbrush

Kitchen paper

Rolling pin

Soft dry cloth

Clear spray varnish (optional)

Techniques

Wet release transfer paper with glue
    (see page 10)

When choosing your canvas, pick one that has been stretched over a
wooden frame or board, giving it a smooth surface texture. Choose a
photograph and enlarge it to approximately 1cm/½in bigger than the
canvas so that it overlaps all four edges. Colour copy the picture on to
the shiny side of a sheet of transfer paper, printing a spare copy in case
of mistakes. Trim any excess paper from your transfer, using either a
scalpel and metal ruler on a cutting mat, or a pair of scissors.

Once you have trimmed the transfer to the correct size, simply lower the image face down, wide edge first, into a large shallow tray of lukewarm water. The paper will start to roll up slightly, but you should allow it to soak for a few minutes until it becomes less opaque.

While the transfer paper is soaking in the water, place the linen canvas frame on a couple of pieces of newspaper and, using a paintbrush, apply a thin coat of 50 per cent water-diluted PVA glue over the whole canvas.

Carefully lift the transfer paper out of the water and lay it face down on a piece of kitchen paper to remove any surface water. Then, using your forefingers and thumbs, slide the backing paper off slightly, leaving one of the long edges exposed, and lay the image face up (glue side down) slightly overlapping the corresponding edge of the canvas. Carefully centre the image and when you are happy with the position, gently place a rolling pin on top and slowly slide the backing paper out from underneath the transfer.

Once the image is in place, look closely and expel any air bubbles with a soft dry cloth or the tip of your finger, to ensure the image is completely flat. Carefully prick any stubborn bubbles with a pin and ease the air out. Fold the overhanging transfer over the sides of the canvas frame.

Leave the canvas art to dry flat for a few hours, then, if you want to achieve a matt finish, apply a thin coat of clear spray varnish, which will also protect the image.

Decorate your bed linen with patterned strips placed edge-to-edge around its border. If you are feeling creative, you could design your own patterns, alternatively a good source of suitable designs are the various copyright-free pattern books that are available (see page 96). These patterns can be copied, and the colours altered to suit the colour scheme of your bedroom.

patterned bed linen

When selecting strips of pattern, remember that longer strips will require you to join fewer pieces together, which will save quite a lot of time. You should also consider whether the fact that the pattern will appear flipped on the bed linen is of any concern (if it contains text, for example). If so, flip the image now so that it will transfer the right way round.

This project uses Epson paper, which allows you to print an image on it direct from an Epson printer. If you do not have a computer, scanner and Epson printer, use the iron-on wet release transfer paper method (see page 10).

You will need

Materials

2 strips of repeatable patterns
    in contrasting colours

Access to a computer, scanner
    and Epson printer

Epson transfer paper

Scalpel and cutting mat, or pair
    of scissors

Plain, pale cotton or cotton-blend
    bed linen

Iron

Marble slab

Baking parchment

Techniques

Epson iron-on transfer paper
    (see page 10)

1 Epson paper can be used on any cotton or cotton blend fabric, but a light-coloured, smooth-textured fabric gives the best results. Calculate how much pattern you will need to cover your bed linen, scan the pattern with a computer scanner and try to fit as many strips as possible on to each sheet of paper. You can print straight on to the Epson transfer paper using the Epson printer. Follow the Epson printer's instructions before printing then, using either a scalpel on a cutting mat or a pair of scissors, cut around the edges of the pattern strips leaving a 5mm/¼in margin along the long edges.

2 Next prepare to iron the pattern on to the edge of the bed linen. Use a marble slab instead of an ironing board – a marble cheese board would be ideal. Place a double layer of ironed scrap material on the marble, then lay the bed linen on top making sure that both are smooth. Use the hottest iron setting suitable for the fabric, but do not use the steam setting. Lay the transfer face down in place and begin ironing, moving slowly from one end to the other using firm pressure and securing all corners.

Once the transfer is secure and the backing paper is cool enough to touch, lift the paper off by peeling it from one end to the other. If a section of pattern has not sealed properly, replace the backing paper and iron over it for a few seconds more.

3 To continue the pattern, repeat step 2 taking care to align the joining edges. When nearing the join, take extra care not to iron over the edge of the paper on to an uncovered image: it would melt and stick to the iron. For extra protection, fold a piece of baking parchment in two and lay it over the seam. Peel off the backing paper, working towards the join.

Apply a second row of pattern in the same way, taking care to keep the two lines parallel.

When all the images are in place, reduce the temperature of the iron slightly, put a piece of baking parchment on top of the lines of pattern and iron all over. This method produces durable, washable results. Remember to turn the bed linen inside-out before laundering.

Protect your favourite shoes

in this stylish linen shoe bag. Take a photograph of your best-loved pair of shoes and transfer it on to the bag creating a chic visual label. In this instance I made the transferred image as close to the actual size of the shoes as possible, just to add extra impact.

As the iron-on process flips the images, you may want to invert the picture before you begin transferring – this is essential if there is any writing on the inside of the shoes.

You could continue the theme of this idea to create laundry bags or even storage bags for treasured items. The finished bags look really pretty hanging casually from a doorknob or a peg on the back of your bedroom door.

You can buy plain-coloured linen or cotton bags of a suitable size for this project, or – if you have time – you could make your own bags. Do remember to use a material made from natural fibres though as these work best with transfers.

linen shoe bag

You will need

Materials

Photograph of a pair of shoes

Access to a colour photocopier

Scalpel and cutting mat, or
　　pair of scissors

Kitchen foil

Linen shoe bag, ironed

Dylon transfer paste

Paintbrush

Iron

Ironing board

Kitchen paper

Rolling pin

Sponge

Bowl

Techniques

Transfer paste (see page 13)

1 Using transfer paste can be messy, so wear old clothes or an apron while working. When choosing your picture, remember that this method will flip the transferred image, so avoid including any text unless you have a computer and scanner to invert the image at this early stage.

Colour copy the photograph on to a sheet of plain paper. Cut out the shoes using either a scalpel on a cutting mat or a pair of scissors. Lay the two shoe images face up on a piece of kitchen foil. Squeeze a generous amount of paste on to each image and, using a paintbrush, spread the paste to completely cover the photocopies.

3 Once the images are completely dry, fill a small bowl with lukewarm water and, using a sponge, soak the paper. Leave for a few minutes. Then, using your fingertip, carefully rub away the paper until the shoes are clearly revealed. Take extra care when rubbing the edges of the image, as these are especially delicate. Leave the shoe bag to dry. Finally, using the paintbrush, apply a thin coat of transfer paste to seal the image. Allow the bag to dry again.

When washing the shoe bag, turn it inside-out and launder on a delicate wash cycle. Always iron the bag on the wrong side – you must never iron directly on the image.

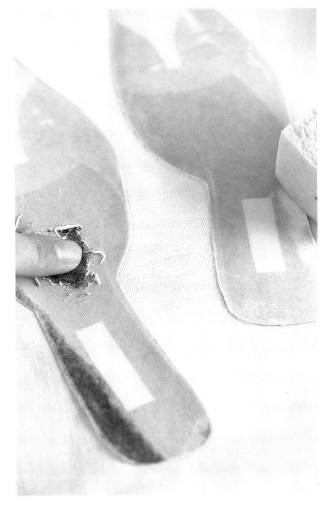

2 Place a piece of kitchen foil inside the linen bag to act as a barrier between the two layers of fabric. Next, when the transfer paste has sunk into the paper, obscuring the images, carefully pick up the first transfer and lay it face down on the fabric. Press the image down firmly, ensuring that there are no wrinkles in the fabric. Then place a piece of kitchen paper on top and, using a rolling pin, lightly press the transfer, rolling in all directions for about a minute to make sure that all the edges have adhered. If any excess paste seeps out, uncover the image and remove the excess paste with kitchen paper. Repeat with the second shoe. Leave to dry for a minimum of four hours but preferably overnight.

Transfers can be overlapped

to give a dramatic, multi-layered effect. It sounds complicated, but is actually very simple. Just pick a coloured background image and a black and white photograph. If you overlap the two images, the white areas of the photograph will take on the colours of the background image. This is a useful method if you want to add colour to a black and white image or if you want to pick out

rose cushion

just a little of the colour scheme of your room. It lets you create subtle colour highlights without the effect becoming overpowering.

For your transfer background, use a simple block of colour, a patterned fabric, or go for something textural such as velvet, wood or distressed copper. Make the background image slightly larger than the rose picture in order to create a casual frame effect.

A set of cushions decorated with roses would make an eye-catching display on a plain sofa or scattered over a bed.

3 When all the pasta shapes are in place around the bowl, leave them to dry for 24 hours. The bowl can then be put in a warm oven (180°C/350°F/gas mark 4) for 10 minutes until the transfers melt and harden into an enamel. This process secures the images and makes them completely water-proof and virtually scratch-proof.

As shown, you don't have to limit yourself to just decorating a serving bowl; you can make a complete set by placing an image in the base of some smaller bowls as well.

Using a close-up picture of a

cactus plant on a glass vase gives the vase's smooth surface the impression of texture. The graphic quality of the transferred cactus looks fantastic on its own, but you could go one step further and fill the vase with some fine sand to give the image more depth of colour.

Use the vase as part of a display, as shown here, by including some thin white candles to

cactus vase

contrast with the beautiful colours of the cactus. Another way to show the pretty purple colour of the vase would be to fill it with glass beads. It would also look great filled with a stylish selection of contemporary sculptural flowers.

If you love plants, but are not blessed with green fingers, this vase is a great way to bring a little extra organic colour into your home without actually having to care for a real plant.

You will need

Materials

Close-up picture of a cactus or other
  plant

Access to a colour photocopier

Large rectangular clear glass vase,
  cleaned to remove any traces
  of grease

Lazertran transfer paper

Kitchen paper

Scalpel, metal ruler and cutting mat,
  or pair of scissors

Large shallow tray

Newspaper

Soft cloth

Oven

Technique

Simple wet release transfer paper
  (see page 10)

1 Enlarge your chosen image until it is big enough to cover at least one side of the vase. If the vase is small enough to allow you to wrap an image around more than one side, then print it large enough to do so and thus avoid unnecessary transfer 'seams' later. Set the toner density to high before colour photocopying on to the shiny side of some transfer paper – this helps to give the image a more solid appearance when applied to glass. Print enough copies to cover the vase, plus an extra in case of mistakes. Trim your transfers to fit neatly on the sides of the vase, using either a scalpel and metal ruler on a cutting mat, or a pair of scissors. Lower the first image face down, wide edge first, into a large shallow tray of lukewarm water. The paper will start to roll up slightly but leave it for a few minutes until it becomes less opaque.

3 When the vase is complete, leave it to dry for 24 hours. Then put it in a warm oven (180°C/350°F/gas mark 4) for about 10 minutes until the transfers melt and harden into an enamel. This will secure the images and make them completely waterproof and virtually scratch-proof.

You can use close-up photos of any plant. Good alternatives are bamboo and grass reeds, as shown below. Their textural qualities make striking vases.

2 Once the transfer paper has been immersed long enough, carefully lift it out of the water and lay it face down on some kitchen paper to remove any excess surface water.

Place the vase on its side on some newspaper. Using your forefingers and thumbs, slide the backing paper off slightly from the top edge and lay the transfer face up (glue side down) along the top edge of the vase. Adjust the position of the image very carefully as transfer paper can tear easily, and make sure that the top edge of the image lines up exactly with the rim of the vase. Then hold the backing paper with one hand and hold down the transfer with the other, and slowly slide the backing paper out from underneath the transfer. Use a soft cloth to expel any air bubbles that appear as you lay the transfer down. Carefully prick any stubborn bubbles with a pin and then gently ease the air out using the tip of your finger.

When you have completed the front of the vase, turn it over and repeat the process on the next side. If you have decided to wrap the transfer around more than one side of the vase, take extra care as you mould the transfer around the corners.

Things are not as they seem

on this witty glass vase. Transfers of goldfish have been used to add a little humour to the design. The fish images are quite intricate, so you may find that cutting them out will be a fiddly job, but the end result is definitely worth the effort.

Continue the theme inside the vase, if you wish, by transferring some pebble images on to the base. As an alternative, you could add a few water plants on the sides of the vase. Let your imagination run wild until you are completely happy with the design, but try not to let the images become cluttered, or you may find that they begin to detract from the flowers you intend to display in the vase.

Here I have half-filled the vase with water and added a few bright orange amaryllis blooms. I like the quirkiness of this arrangement, since the idea of fish swimming around the flower stems appeals to my sense of humour. It looks just as good if you fill the vase with water and simply float a few flower heads on the surface.

fishbowl vase

You will need

Materials

Pictures of 2 goldfish (see page 88)

Access to a colour photocopier

Lazertran transfer paper

Scalpel and cutting mat, or pair
  of scissors

Clear glass globe vase

Masking tape

Shallow bowl

Sponge

Kitchen paper

Oven

Technique

Simple wet release transfer paper
  (see page 10)

1 Colour photocopy the two goldfish images on to the shiny side of a sheet of transfer paper. You may want to include some extra copies, in case of mistakes. Set the photocopier's toner density to high – this will help to give the images a more solid appearance when they are transferred on to glass. To use transfer paper on non-absorbent shiny surfaces like glass, no glue is needed other than the gum on the back of the paper but, before you start transferring, clean the surface to remove any traces of grease. Carefully trim your transfers to size using either a scalpel on a cutting mat, or a pair of scissors.

3 When the vase is complete, allow it to dry for 24 hours. It can then be put in a warm oven (180°C/350°F/gas mark 4) for about 10 minutes until the transfers melt and harden into an enamel. This secures the images and makes them completely waterproof and virtually scratch-proof.

You could add more fish or other images such as pebbles. The pebble image shown below was placed inside the vase, which can be tricky to access. This sort of intricate work is best done in two or four sections. Cut round the pebbles and join them one at a time – it will not matter if they overlap slightly.

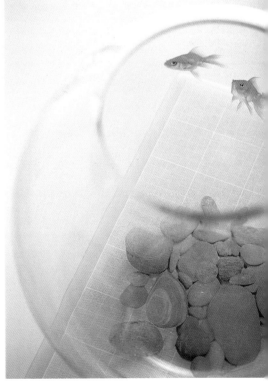

2 Mark where you want to position the goldfish images by temporarily sticking them on to the surface of the vase with pieces of masking tape. When you are happy with their positions, place the transfers face down in a shallow bowl of lukewarm water; alternatively you can soak them individually with a wet sponge. Leave the masking tape in place on the vase to mark where you want the transfers to go. The paper will start to roll up slightly but leave the transfers to soak for a few minutes until the paper becomes less opaque.

Carefully lift the first transfer out of the bowl and lay it face down on some kitchen paper to remove the excess surface water. Place the vase in front of you, carefully pick up the transfer and, using your forefinger and thumb, slide a little of the backing paper off. Lay the image face up (glue side down) in position on the vase. Then carefully pull the backing paper out from underneath the transfer, and, if necessary, adjust the position of the image. Expel any air bubbles using the tip of your finger. Repeat with the second fish.

Add a personal touch with

this beautifully decorated plastic tissue box cover – a less fussy alternative to the traditional frilly lace cover. Choose a design for your tissue box that will co-ordinate with the décor of your room or complement the other items on your dressing table, creating a unified look.

The pictures you use could be just one image repeated on each side of the box or a number of different images. You could photograph your favourite bottles of perfume and transfer the results on to the sides of the box, as shown here. I chose a simple antique perfume bottle for this project because I like its elegant lines, but you could use pictures of the bottles you keep on your dressing table. Alternatively, you could use a photograph of some jewellery, or perhaps some shapely lipsticks and make-up brushes.

You could take this project a step further and decorate other containers, such as a child's toy box or a useful desk-tidy for the home office.

tissue box

You will need

Materials

4 square images of scent bottles
(see page 92)

Access to a colour photocopier

Lazertran transfer paper

Scalpel, metal ruler and cutting mat,
or pair of scissors

Plastic box, cleaned to remove any
traces of grease

Large shallow bowl

Kitchen paper

Soft cloth (optional)

Clear spray varnish

Technique

Simple wet release transfer paper
(see page 10)

1 Most square tissue boxes measure 11.5cm/4½ in on all sides, but it is wise to measure your tissue box before you begin. Your plastic box must be slightly larger than the tissue box so that the tissue box can fit inside it.

When you have chosen which images you want to feature on the tissue box cover, enlarge or reduce them until they are slightly bigger than one side of the box. Colour photocopy the images on to the shiny side of some transfer paper.

Using either a scalpel and metal ruler on a cutting mat, or a pair of scissors, trim any excess paper from the transfers. Take care, as transfer paper is very delicate and can tear easily.

To use transfer paper on non-absorbent shiny surfaces like plastic, no glue is needed other than the gum on the back of the paper. Place one of the trimmed images face down in a large shallow bowl filled with lukewarm water and leave it to soak. The paper will start to roll up slightly but leave it for a few minutes until it becomes less opaque.

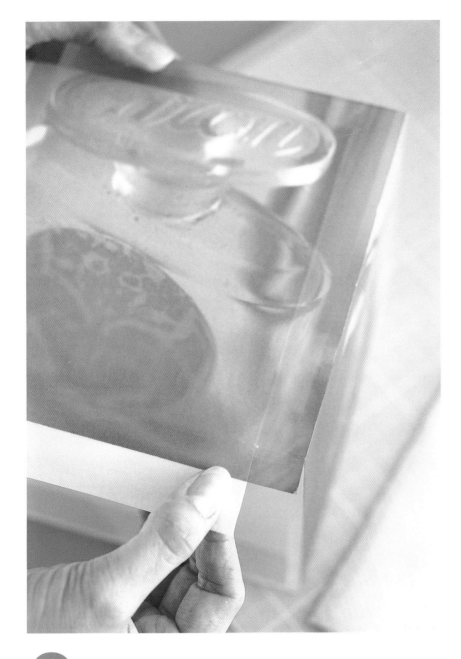

2 Carefully lift the first transfer out of the water and lay it face down on some kitchen paper to remove the surface water. Place the box on its side in front of you, then with your forefingers and thumbs carefully slide the backing paper off slightly from one corner and lay the transfer face up (glue side down) centrally on the side of the box.

Hold the backing paper with one hand and hold down the transfer with the other and gradually slide the backing paper out from under the transfer. Expel any air bubbles with a soft dry cloth or the tip of your finger. Run the blade of a scalpel along the edges of the tissue box to neatly trim off the overhanging edges of the transfer paper.

Repeat the process to cover the remaining three sides of the box then leave it to dry for 24 hours. Once the transfers are completely dry, spray the box with varnish to protect it from becoming scratched.

3 You can adapt the idea behind this project to other household containers. A simple make-up box, for example, looks great decorated with images of lipsticks and brushes.

Whatever container you make, you will probably find it useful to add a protective layer of spray varnish, particularly if the container is used frequently.

This project works equally well

on a metal or plastic tray, but a light-coloured background is usually the most effective as it contrasts with the transferred images. Since transfer paper is so thin, it lends pictures an element of translucency. This characteristic can be used to allow a patterned or textured background, such as the wood of this tray, to show through the lightest areas of the pictures. In this case the man's white shirt takes on the grain and colour of the wood. The warm tones mix well with the original colours of the photograph giving a sepia-like result.

I chose a series of four pictures for this project, but repeating one image would work as well. The images can be neatly arranged in a rectangle in the centre of the tray, as seen here, but it would be equally interesting to place them in a straight line, thus drawing attention to the sequence of movements shown in the photographs.

Alternatively, you could let your imagination go wild and use overlayed images of different sizes to cover the tray.

take-away tray

You will need

Materials

4 action shots (see page 91)

Access to a colour photocopier

Lazertran transfer paper

Scalpel, metal ruler and cutting mat,
    or pair of scissors

Wooden tray

Ruler

Masking tape

2 shallow bowls

Pure turpentine

Small sponge roller

Kitchen paper

Soft dry cloth

Pump-action spray bottle (optional)

Clear spray varnish (optional)

Technique

Wet-release transfer paper with
    turpentine (see page 10)

1 First choose a series of four photographs – action shots work particularly well. Here pictures of a chef taking advantage of a few spare moments to eat his lunch have been used.

As this technique uses turpentine, wear old clothes or an apron and make sure that the room is well ventilated. Copy your chosen pictures on to the shiny side of a sheet of transfer paper. Trim all four images to the same size using either a scalpel and metal ruler on a cutting mat, or a pair of scissors. Use a ruler to measure where the pictures should go in order to sit right in the centre of the tray. The four pictures should fit edge to edge to make a large rectangle.

3 Repeat the transfer process with the remaining three images. Once the pictures are in place and you have removed all of the air bubbles, leave the tray to dry flat overnight. You will then notice that the transfers will begin to melt and sink (migrate) into the surface.

When the transfers are almost dry, you will be able to judge how well they have set. If necessary, spray them with a fine mist of turpentine to finish off the process. A pump-action spray bottle is ideal for this job. Take care not to apply too much turpentine or the images will break up.

If you are likely to use the tray regularly, it is a good idea to apply a thin layer of clear spray varnish as this will protect the transfers from becoming scratched. Apply the varnish before you remove the masking tape from the surface of the tray.

2 Once you have measured where the four pictures will go, mask around all four sides of the collage area with strips of masking tape, leaving a blank space in the centre of the tray where the images will be placed. Then lower the images one at a time into a shallow bowl of lukewarm water. The transfers will start to roll up but allow them to soak for a few minutes until they become less opaque.

Meanwhile pour some pure turpentine into a second shallow bowl and, using a sponge roller, lightly roll a thin layer of turpentine on to the masked-off area in the centre of the tray. Lift the transfers out of the water and lay them face down on kitchen paper to remove any excess water. Using your forefingers and thumbs, ease a bit of the backing paper off and lay the first image face up (glue side down) in position. Carefully slide out the backing paper while smoothing out any bubbles using a soft dry cloth.

As transfers tear easily and stick to turpentine quite quickly, take extra care not to break the image if you need to adjust its position.

If you look to nature when designing your projects, you will find that it helps you to find harmonious colour combinations. The autumn colour palette, when leaves are turning, can be absolutely stunning. The skeletal leaves used in this project have a beautiful cobweb-like delicacy, but you don't have to wait until the autumn to collect them, as most craft shops and some gift shops sell them in small packs.

autumnal lampshade

The paper stretching technique explained in this project is necessary whenever you use wet release transfers on paper; it stops the paper wrinkling when the wet transfer is applied. The process is actually very simple, but it does involve a little preparation.

Paper stretching involves a type of gum tape, which becomes sticky when dampened. It is used to tape damp paper to a stiff board and dries at the same rate as the paper while the board keeps everything flat. For details of where to buy gum tape, please refer to the suppliers section on page 96.

You will need

Materials

Scalpel, metal ruler and cutting mat

Sheet of heavy watercolour paper

Cylindrical wire lampshade frame

Large wooden board

Gum tape

Sponge

Skeletal leaf (or see page 86)

Access to a colour photocopier

Lazertran transfer paper

2 small bowls

50 per cent water-diluted PVA glue

Paintbrush

Kitchen paper

Soft dry cloth

Double-sided sticky tape

Fire-resistant spray

Technique

Water release transfer paper with glue
  (see page 10)

1 As this technique involves the use of PVA glue, wear old clothes or an apron while working. First, using a scalpel and metal ruler, cut the watercolour paper to a size about 2cm/¾in larger than you will need to wrap around the wire lampshade frame.

Next stretch your paper. To do this, first lay the watercolour paper on a large wooden board, leaving a border of at least 10cm/4in all round. Next, dampen the glued side of the gum tape and stick it firmly along all the edges of the paper (about 2cm/¾in from the edge). The gum tape will secure the paper to the board. Using a sponge, wet the paper and gum tape. The paper will start to ripple, but this is fine.

Leave the paper overnight by which time it will be completely flat again. Meanwhile, work out your design for the lampshade.

2 Calculate how many leaf images you will need to cover the whole of the lampshade, then try to fit them all on to one sheet of paper – you could use a computer and scanner to aid this process, or simply colour photocopy the leaves a number of times, then cut them out and stick them on a blank sheet of paper.

Change the colour of the leaves if you wish. This can be done by scanning the leaf images and manipulating the colour with a computer or, to a lesser extent, by altering the colour levels on a colour photocopier. Colour copy the sheet of leaves on to the shiny side of some transfer paper.

Carefully cut out the leaf images using a scalpel on a cutting mat. Pour some 50 per cent water-diluted PVA glue in to a small bowl and brush a thin layer on to the paper.

3 Place a couple of leaves into a bowl of lukewarm water and leave them to soak for a few minutes until the paper becomes less opaque and curls up. One at a time carefully lift the transfers out of the water and lay them face down on some kitchen paper to remove any excess moisture. Using your forefinger and thumb, begin to slide the backing paper off and position the tip of the leaf face up (glue side down) on the tacky paper, then slowly slide out the backing paper from underneath the transfer. Expel any air bubbles with the tip of your finger to ensure the image has adhered completely. Prick any stubborn bubbles with a pin and ease the air out with a soft dry cloth or your fingers. Repeat with the remaining leaves then allow to dry.

When dry, using a scalpel and metal ruler, trim the gum tape from around all four edges of the sheet of paper. Lay it face down on a table and place the wire lampshade frame on top, then wrap the paper around the frame and join the seam with some double-sided sticky tape. For safety, coat the lampshade inside and out with some fire-resistant spray.

Forget boring labels on your kitchen storage tins and go for images instead. What else could be contained in this canister but the tastiest selection of cookies? This project provides the perfect way to smarten up your tins and add interest to your kitchen.

As cookie tins are always in and out of the cupboard especially if you have a young family – baking the tin in a warm oven to render the

cookie tin

transfer waterproof and virtually scratch-proof is a very good idea. Try to find a tin without a rubber seal under the lid as this is unsuitable for the oven. Alternatively, just decorate the main container and leave the lid unadorned.

You could extend this idea to other storage tins; a jar of coffee beans or a tea caddy, for example. If you intend to use the pictures as labels, then try to select easily identifiable images. Alternatively, use text – you certainly wouldn't want to reach for a jar of sugar and end up with salt!

You will need

Materials

Pictures of cookies (see page 89)

Access to a colour photocopier

Lazertran transfer paper

Scalpel and cutting mat, or pair
   of scissors

Large shallow bowl

Metal cookie tin, cleaned to remove
   any traces of grease

Soft cloth

Kitchen paper

Oven

Technique

Simple wet release transfer paper
   (see page 10)

1 Colour photocopy both the picture of the stack of cookies and the single cookie making sure they will fit on the side and lid of the biscuit tin respectively. Set the toner density to high and colour photocopy the images on to the shiny side of a sheet of transfer paper – this gives the images a more solid appearance when applied to metal. Print a couple of copies in case of mistakes, then trim around the edge of the cookies using either a scalpel on a cutting mat, or a pair of scissors.

2 Once trimmed simply lower the cookie images, face down, into a large shallow bowl filled with lukewarm water and leave them to soak. The paper will start to roll up slightly, but leave the transfers for a few minutes until they become less opaque. Once they have soaked, carefully lift the transfers out of the water and lay them face down on some kitchen paper to remove any surface water.

3 Place the metal tin on its side on a soft cloth to stop it rolling around while you are positioning the transfer. Gently ease off the backing paper from the large transfer and, remembering that the image can slide, carefully position it face up (glue side down) on the side of the cookie tin. Once the image is in place, carefully expel any air bubbles using a soft cloth. Do the same with the picture of the single cookie, placing it on the lid.

Leave the two cookie transfers to dry for about 24 hours. Then, leaving the tin open, put it in a warm oven (180°C/350°F/gas mark 4) for approximately 10 minutes until the transfers melt and harden into an enamel. The heat process secures the transferred images, making them completely waterproof and virtually scratch-proof.

Organic materials have a simple beauty that complements most interiors. Just light the candle in this cubic stone holder and watch the shadows play across the room.

The Latin phrases on the sides of the candle holder give the illusion of having been carved into the surface of the stone, but this is not the case. By using transfers on stone, you can easily achieve an authentic engraved look. Do try to choose a pale stone, however, as this will help improve the text's legibility. I have used some Latin phrases in this project, but you could use phrases from any language.

Some stone is quite rough so you might need to apply a misting of turpentine to make sure the transfer has totally adhered into the surface, nevertheless, the technique is very easy.

Since this candle holder has four sides, you could choose expressions to suit your changing mood, so you might have a quotation or maxim that will cheer you up on one side, calm you down on another, and so on. Simply light a candle and turn the candle holder to the side you find most appropriate to your mood.

stone candle holder

You will need

Materials

Latin phrases (see page 93)

Access to a colour photocopier

Lazertran transfer paper

Scalpel, metal ruler and cutting mat,
   or pair of scissors

2 shallow bowls

Kitchen paper

Pure turpentine

Small sponge roller

Cube-shaped stone candle holder

Soft cloth

Pump-action spray bottle

Technique

Wet release transfer paper with turpentine
   (see page 10)

1 Choose an attractive font and type out the words you want to appear on the candle holder. The Latin sentences used in this project are *imperium Oceano, famam qui terminet astris,* taken from the *Aeneid,* meaning 'The Empire of Ocean, whose fame reached to the stars'; *si tu vales, ego gaudeo,* which translates as 'If you are well, I am pleased'; and *ut seritur, ita metitur, which means* 'As one sows, so does one reap'.

As this technique uses turpentine, wear old clothes or an apron while you are working and make sure that the room is well ventilated. Fit your chosen phrases on to a sheet of paper and photocopy the sheet of phrases on to the shiny side of some transfer paper. Print a couple more copies than you expect to use in case of mistakes. Using either a scalpel, metal ruler and cutting mat, or a pair of scissors, trim around the text so that each phrase will fit on to one side of the candle holder.

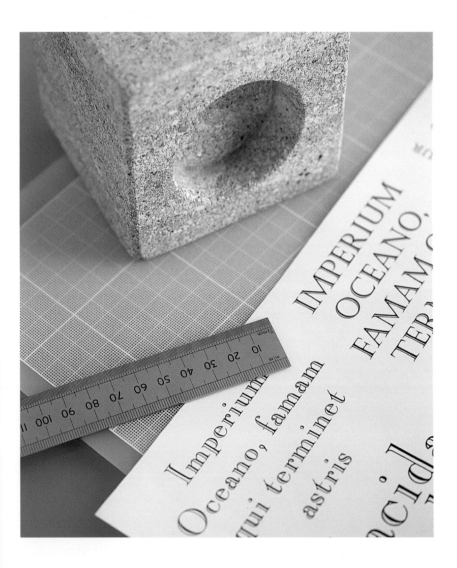

2 Once you have decided on the position of your text, lower the first transfer into a shallow bowl of lukewarm water. The paper will start to roll up but leave it to soak for a few minutes until it becomes less opaque. Lift the transfer out of the water and lay it face down on a piece of kitchen paper to remove any excess water. Meanwhile pour some pure turpentine into another bowl and use the sponge roller to apply the turpentine to one side of the candle holder.

3 Lift the transfer off the kitchen paper, then with your forefingers and thumbs, slide the backing paper off slightly. Lay the transfer face up (glue side down) on the surface you have turpentined and carefully slide out the backing paper. Once the text is in place, using a soft dry cloth, make sure the image is flat and secure with no air bubbles, then leave to dry, lying flat. The transfer will start to melt and sink (migrate) into the surface.

As the stone surface is quite rough, pour a little turpentine into a pump-action spray bottle and mist the transfer. Do not to spray the text too closely, as too much turpentine will make the transfer break up. Repeat steps 2 and 3 with the remaining transfers. Once dry, the candle holder is ready for use.

Place mats are perfect for

transfers – they are flat, and therefore easy to work on, and they look lovely on a table set for a meal. You can purchase blanks – place mats that have already been cut and shaped – or you can make your own quite simply using MDF. The etching process used in this project is very simple to carry out, and a final coat of varnish will protect the mats for years to come.

floral place mats

The simple floral design used here, created from a pressed flower, provides a wonderful way to bring the garden into your home, or to give a constant memory of a special flower you grew or were given. Instead of repeating a single motif on all six mats, you could choose six related images that complement each other, such as six types of flower or six different leaves. You could also make a matching serving mat and some coasters to complete your set if you wish.

You will need

Materials

6 MDF place mats

Pale paint primer

2 tester pots of fast-drying water-based
    paint

Flat-ended 2.5cm/1in paintbrush

Pressed flower or picture of a pressed
    flower (see page 87)

Access to a colour photocopier

Lazertran transfer paper

Scalpel and cutting mat, or pair
    of scissors

2 shallow bowls

Pure turpentine

Small sponge roller

Kitchen paper

Clear spray varnish

Technique

Wet release transfer paper with turpentine
    (see page 10)

1 As this project involves the use of paint and turpentine, wear old clothes or an apron while you are working and make sure that the room is well ventilated. Paint each place mat with a coat of primer on one side and on all four edges. Once the primer is dry, paint the place mats with two coats of fast-drying water-based paint in your chosen back-ground colour, allowing the mats to dry between each coat.

2 Fit six colour copies of the flower on to one sheet of paper – you could use a computer and scanner to aid this process or you could colour photocopy the flower six times, cut them out and stick them all on a blank sheet of paper.

Colour copy the sheet of images on to the shiny side of a piece of transfer paper. Carefully cut out the flowers from the transfer paper using either a scalpel on a cutting mat, or a pair of scissors.

3 Pour a little pure turpentine into a small shallow bowl and, using a sponge roller, prepare the surface of the first place mat by applying a thin layer of turpentine to the area where the transfer will be positioned.

Place the first cut-out image face down in a bowl of lukewarm water and leave it until the paper becomes less opaque. Lift the transfer out carefully, as transfer paper tears easily, especially if the image is very delicate. Place it face down on some kitchen paper to remove any surface water. Ease off the backing paper between your forefinger and thumb.

4 Depending on the intricacy of the image, use either your fingers or the tip of a scalpel to position the image face up (glue side down) on the mat. Gently remove any air bubbles with your fingertips and leave to dry overnight. The transfer will melt and sink (migrate) into the surface of the mat. Repeat this process with the remaining place mats. Try to avoid overusing the turpentine, as this can cause the image to disintegrate. Once the image has dried, coat the place mats with a layer of clear matt spray varnish to protect them.

Display your child's artwork

in a new and entertaining way. This project shows you how to decorate a plain office object in a way that will remind you of your children.

You could ask your child to draw a self-portrait or even a picture of what he or she thinks you look like. Alternatively, you could photocopy and transfer a special piece of artwork that your child has already completed.

Objects decorated with a child's drawing make great presents – your relatives will treasure them. Plain mouse mats are inexpensive and available from stationers and office suppliers.

The technique used in this project is simple to accomplish, but since a mouse mat needs to have an absolutely smooth surface you will need to be especially careful to squeeze out all the air bubbles after you have removed the transfer's backing paper. If the mat begins to curl, wait until it dries and then place it under some heavy books for a few hours so that the computer mouse will be able to glide easily over its surface when you come to use it.

mouse mat

You will need

Materials

Child's drawing
Access to a colour photocopier
Lazertran transfer paper
Scalpel and cutting mat, or pair
    of scissors
Large shallow tray
Pure turpentine
Small shallow bowl
Small sponge roller
Kitchen paper
Plastic mouse mat
Rolling pin

Technique

Wet release transfer paper with
    turpentine (see page 10)

3 Lift the transfer off the kitchen paper, then with your forefingers and thumbs carefully slide the backing paper off slightly and lay the image face up (glue side down) on the mouse mat. Carefully slide out the backing paper and adjust the transfer's position. Use a rolling pin, in one direction only, to make sure that the image is secure with no trapped air bubbles. Leave the mat to dry flat overnight. The transfer will sink (migrate) into the surface of the mouse mat and it is then ready for use.

1 As this technique involves the use of turpentine, wear some old clothes or an apron when you are working and make sure that the room is well ventilated. Colour copy the child's drawing, enlarging it or reducing it as necessary, so that it fully fits the surface of your mouse mat. Then, colour copy it on to the shiny side of some transfer paper. Trim your transfer to size, using either a scalpel on a cutting mat, or a pair of scissors.

2 Lower your image into a large shallow tray filled with lukewarm water. The paper will start to curl up slightly but leave it to soak for a few minutes until it becomes less opaque. Pour some pure turpentine into a small shallow bowl and, using a sponge roller, apply a thin layer of turpentine on to the surface of the mouse mat. Carefully lift the transfer out of the water and lay it face down on a piece of kitchen paper to remove any excess water.

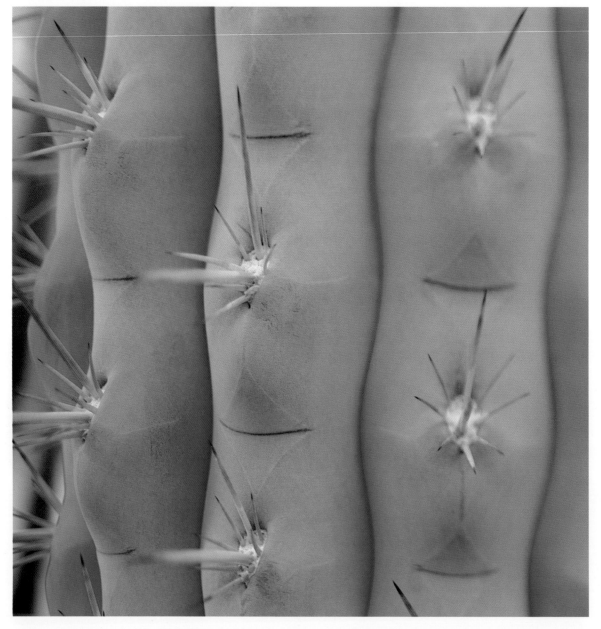

IMPERIUM OCEANO FAMAM QUI TERMINET ASTRIS

si tu vales, ego gaudeo

ut seritur, ita metitur

Page numbers in **bold** refer to the projects; illustrations are indicated in *italic*.

First published in 2001
by Conran Octopus Limited
a part of Octopus Publishing Group
2–4 Heron Quays
London E14 4JP

www.conran-octopus.co.uk

Text copyright © 2001 Conran
Octopus Limited
Project designs copyright © 2001
Isabel de Cordova
Book design and layout copyright
© 2001 Conran Octopus Limited
Photography copyright © 2001
Conran Octopus Limited

ISBN 1 84091 018 6

The publishers have made every
effort to ensure that all instructions
given in this book are accurate, but
cannot accept liability for any
resulting loss or damage, whether
direct or consequential and
howsoever arising.

Publishing Director Lorraine Dickey
Commissioning Editor Emma Clegg
Senior Editor Katey Day
Editorial Assistant Ellie Hutt

Creative Director Leslie Harrington
Designer Nicky Collings
Photographer Sue Wilson
Stylists Isabel de Cordova and
Emily Jewsbury
Production Director Zoe Fawcett
Senior Production Controller
Manjit Sihra

Author's Acknowledgements
This book is dedicated to my mother,
Gillian de Cordova.

A big thank you to my family and
friends who all gave me invaluable
support in the creation of this book.
I would also like to acknowledge the
help of the team at Conran Octopus
for providing me with this opportunity
to publish my first book.

Suppliers

Most art shops will stock canvases,
turpentine, PVA glue and spray
varnishes and some might stock
Lazertran or Epson transfer paper and
Dylon transfer paste. Most large
haberdasheries sell Dylon products.
Alternatively, you could contact the
manufacturer for details of your
nearest stockist.

Lazertran Ltd
(Wet release transfer paper)
8 Alban Square
Aberaeron
Dyfed SA46 0AD
Tel: 01545 571149
Website: www.lazertran.com
Email: mic@lazertran.com

You can use Lazertran with the
following printers: Canon, Xerox,
Minolta, Ricoh (but not Hewlett
Packard).

Epson UK Ltd
(Iron on transfer paper)
Campus 100
Maylands Avenue
Hemel Hemstead
Hertfordshire HP2 7TJ
Tel: 01442 261144
Website: www.epson.co.uk
Email: enquiry@epson.co.uk
You can use Epson Transfer paper with
the following printers: Epson Stylus
Colour 400, 600, 800 and Epson Stylus
Photo.

Dylon – Colour fun image maker –
(Fabric paste)
Dylon International Limited
Worsley Bridge Road
Lower Sydenham
London SE26 5HD
Tel: 020 8663 4801
Website: www.dylon.co.uk

The Color Co.
(Colour photocopiers across Britain.
Note – They will charge a computer
set-up fee if printing from disk.)
Website: www.colorco.com

London Graphic Centre
(Art supplies)
16–18 Shelton Street
London WC2H 9JJ
Tel: 020 7759 4500

The Dover Bookshop
(Suppliers of copyright-free images)
18 Earlham St
London WC2H 9LG
Tel: 020 7836 2111
Website: www.doverbooks.co.uk

Brodie and Middleton
(for Brogard Flame Retardant Spray)
68 Drury Lane
London WC2B 5SP
Tel: 020 7836 3289
Email: info@RandC.net
Flame retardant spray is also available
from DIY shops

Shops
(for inexpensive plain objects to use in
the projects)

Ikea
branches nationwide
Website: www.ikea.co.uk

Habitat
Website: www.habitat.net (lists branch
locations throughout the UK)

Companies that supply MDF blanks
(for use in the place mats project):

Scumble Goosie
Lewiston Mill
Toadsmoor Road
Brimscombe, Stroud
Gloucestershire GL5 2TB
Tel: 01453 731305
Website: www.scumble-goosie.co.u

Paint Magic
79 Shepperton Road
London N1 3DF
Tel: 020 7354 9696

Credits
Fork P1, P12 and P14 – Dover
Publishing
Fob watch P15 – Dover publishing
Picture of Children (Paula and
Marc Landau) P19, P26, P28 and
P29 – Alistair Blair
Bedlinen pattern P31, P32 and
P33 – Dover publishing
Cactus, Bamboo and Grass Reeds
P53– copyright © Octopus Publishin
Group/Peter Myers
Perfume image P58, P60 and P61 –
copyright © Octopus Publishing
Group/Sandra Lane
Chef images P63, P64, P65 – copyri
© Octopus Publishing Group/
Sandra Lane
Child's drawing P83, P84 and P85 –
Heather Dunleavy